KETTLEBELL WORKOUT

Effective Kettlebell Workouts to Help You Lose Weight

(The Complete Kettlebell Workout to Losing Weight)

Marilyn Guan

Published by Tomas Edwards

© **Marilyn Guan**

All Rights Reserved

Kettlebell Workout: Effective Kettlebell Workouts to Help You Lose Weight (The Complete Kettlebell Workout to Losing Weight)

ISBN 978-1-990268-64-9

Legal & Disclaimer

The information contained in this book is not designed to replace or take the place of any form of medicine or professional medical advice. The information in this book has been provided for educational and entertainment purposes only.

The information contained in this book has been compiled from sources deemed reliable, and it is accurate to the best of the Author's knowledge; however, the Author cannot guarantee its accuracy and validity and cannot be held liable for any errors or omissions. Changes are periodically made to this book. You must consult your doctor or get professional medical advice before using any of the suggested remedies, techniques, or information in this book.

Table of Contents

Introduction

Before you delve into the world of kettlebell training to find out how to achieve increased strength and muscle with kettlebell workouts, you must ask yourself, what is a kettlebell? Well, a kettlebell is a cast iron or cast steel weight used mainly in ballistic exercises that combine cardiovascular, strength and flexibility trainings. This is the main piece of equipment in the weight lifting discipline of girevoy.

The kettlebell originated in Russia in the 1700s, when farmers used to use kettlebells to help weigh their crops. After a while though, it is said that the farmers realized that they were getting stronger, and they found out that these new weights they were using on their crops were perfect for showcasing their new found strength. They started off competing in local trade fairs and festivals;

but by the 1900s, the sport was being practiced all over Eastern Europe. It was so popular and so effective at conditioning the body that even the soviet military used kettlebells as part of their physical training and conditioning regime.

There are many different kettlebell workouts, with all of them aimed at increasing strength and endurance. They focus mainly on the shoulders, lower back and legs of an individual, though many are mainly holistic exercises, focusing on the whole body. The basic movements of kettlebell exercises tend to mimic real world activities, such as farm work or digging, making this the ideal weight to use for those looking for a full body workout.

Kettlebell workouts are very aerobic in comparison to more conventional weight training techniques. There are more repetitions per exercise, and sets last longer, with breaks being shorter in duration than with normal weight training exercises done with bars or with dumbbells. The holistic nature of these exercises and the intensity of kettlebell training means that the exercises should not be taken lightly. It has been suggested that if you are new to kettlebell training, you should start out slowly, building up the pace as you continue to allow your body time to acclimatize itself to the new training regime. If you suffer from shoulder or back injuries, extra precautions should be taken to avoid aggravating and exiting injury, or causing further injury to yourself.

This book promises to explore the many different kettlebell training techniques and the different benefits that these techniques can offer. It shall explore the different avenues that can be taken to get the most out of a kettlebell, to achieve your target fitness or dream body.

Kettlebells are so versatile in their use, it is important to first look at the four different general ways or styles you can use to train with them.

1. Hardstyle.

This style is heavily influenced by Powerlifting. It focuses mainly on the duality of relaxation and tension and the build-up of strength during training.

2.Girevoy

Also called fluid style; this is the style used when training for competitive kettlebell lifting championships.

3.Crossfit

This workout refers to the use of the kettlebell in the crossfit curriculum.

4.Juggling

As the name suggests, this method of kettlebell training involves throwing and catching the kettlebell, while different tricks are performed with it.

These four techniques can be used separately or all together depending on what effect you would like to have on your body and which muscle groups you would like to focus on. In this guide, you shall get a walkthrough to the different exercises that can be done with a kettlebell, what style they use (keeping in mind that the styles are quite similar, other than the juggling style), and what muscle groups these different exercises target.

An important point to note is that as with all exercise regimes, the exercises in this book should be done around some sort of supervision at the onset to help ensure that the drills are being done properly. Flying solo and doing these exercises by yourself in the comfort of your home or gym may be the end game, but never underestimate the wealth of knowledge a consummate professional can bring to the table. After all, even a natural flier like a hummingbird needs to be taught how to fly.

Chapter 1: How To Choose A Kettlebell

According to a study conducted at the University of Wisconsin- La Crosse, there are so many ways in which you can choose a kettlebell. Mostly, the kettlebells vary in designs. There are those that are coated with rubber to protect the floors from the resulting impact. Other designs are designed specifically for competitions. Such kettlebells have a straight handle and are uniform in shape and size irrespective of the weight.

Over the years, some manufacturers have designed kettlebells with a concave face for ergonomic factors. Others like the newfangled kettlebells work the same way as dumbbells, which means that they can be loaded with plates for weight adjustments with just a single implement. For instance, kettlebell swings and getups are said to get the heart rate up and burn more fats in the same manner a cardio machine does but can do more in re-enforcing good mechanics.

Therefore, if you plan on buying your first kettlebell, it is important that you do the test before making the purchase. Start by holding up your hand and touch your thumb to the tip of your pinkie. Take note of the channel that forms on your palm. This is the point at which the kettlebell handle is supposed to rest most of the time. That is from the outside knuckle of your index finger down to the opposite side of your wrist in a diagonal orientation.

Follow this by picking up the weight and then holding the handle in the middle so that it fills the channel. Ensure that the bell rests on the back of your forearm and that the wrist at this point is straight. It is important that it does not impinge on the boney profile of your wrist. If at some point you pick up the kettlebell

and it rubs against the bone protruding on the lateral side of your wrist, then this means that the weight displacement from the handle is not ideal. In other words, there is a high risk of you getting injured.

The best safety tip at this point is for you to avoid choosing a kettlebell that has a thick handle. You will realize that Onnit's handles have a diameter that is a little over an inch. This is enough when it comes to working your grip strength, while not causing unnecessary fatigue.

When performing an exercise like a swing, there is a possibility that you will be making so many reps in a single workout. The key here is to ensure that your grip does not burn out. This is mainly because it is counterproductive from a technical standpoint. When the grip is overworked, there is a chance that you will see a whole slew of mechanical problems that will occur. As for how much weight you should begin with, men can typically lift 16 kilos while women can lift 8 kilos.

Chapter 2: Heart Rate

How to Measure Heart Rate?

It is important for an individual to calculate the heart rate as unusually low or high heart rate indicates a health problem. For this purpose, the simple way to calculate the heart rate through pulse, which is common, found in the wrist, inside elbow, side of the neck and top of the foot. Few steps help to calculate accurate heart rate:

Step 1: The first step is to relax your body and find a comfortable place. It is crucial that an individual is not restless and stay motionless for at least five to ten minutes.

Step 2: Once the body is relaxed, find the radial artery or pulse in the relevant place and apply pressure with the index or middle fingers.

Step 3: After this, count the number of beats an individual feel for ten seconds with the help of a digital watch.

Step 4: This process should be repeated three to four times to find the accurate heart rate and find the average number. Now multiply this number by six to achieve the RHR.

Step 5: It is essential to have regular check up to keep a track and ensure that a healthy RHR is maintained.

In case, the resting heart rate is consistently above 100 then it is essential to consult a doctor to avoid any severe problem. Moreover, if an individual is not involved in any strenuous physical activities like trained athletes then it is a sign of a problem. Especially if an individual suffers from constant dizziness, shortness of breath or fainting. On contrary, researchers depict that a heart rate below than 60 may be due to the usage of drugs. Moreover, athletic people or active people tend to have a lower heart rate as their muscles are efficient and are in good condition, which requires fewer efforts. Whereas, a person who is relatively less active or has a sedentary lifestyle might have a heart rate between 60 and 100 as the muscles have to work more to maintain bodily functions.

Target Heart Rates

Various factors influence the heart rate such as inactivity, bad eating habits and negative lifestyle behaviors such as excessive use of drugs or smoking. Moreover, heart rate is also influenced by overall fitness and health level of an individual. Other than this, researchers indicate that age is also an important factor that affects the heart rate as young hearts works faster and efficiently than people who aged above 60.

It is suggested that it is essential to measure your heart rate to gain benefits and improve heart health. A person's target heart rate zone is between 50 percent and 85 percent of his or her maximum heart rate. The most common way to calculate is by subtracting your age from 220. For example, a person who aged 30 can subtract it from 220, which will give 190. Now target zone for a 30-year-old person would be between 50 and 85 percent of his or her maximum heart rate so multiply 190 x 0.50 and 190 x 0.85, which will give 95 bpm and 162 bpm respectively. However, for people are above 40 are suggested to subtract 10.75 multiply age from 208 as the other formula can overestimate the maximum heart rate.

In addition, an adult's age can compensate for their slower hearts by making the most of every beat. A bigger, more powerful heart compensates for a slower speed by moving more blood with each stroke. The goal of exercise in older adults

Age	Target HR Zone 50-85%	Average Maximum Heart Rate, 100%
20 years	100-170 beats per minute	200 beats per minute
30 years	95-162 beats per minute	190 beats per minute

35 years	93-157 beats per minute		185 beats per minute
40 years	90-153 beats per minute		180 beats per minute
45 years	88-149 beats per minute		175 beats per minute
50 years	85-145 beats per minute		170 beats per minute
55 years	83-140 beats per minute		165 beats per minute
60 years	80-136 beats per minute		160 beats per minute
65 years	78-132 beats per minute		155 beats per minute
70 years	75-128 beats per minute		150 beats per minute

Chapter 3: The 13 Soviet Kettlebell Moves

Kettlebell Exercise No.1: Kettle Halo

The kettlebell halo, also known as "around the world", is an excellent exercise for core development, and shoulder strength. Grab the kettlebell from the outside of the horns, and bring it up to chin level, so that you are holding it upside down in a goblet squat position. The bottom of the kettlebell should be facing the ceiling. The elbows should be tucked in, in a rack position. Now drive the elbows to one side, so that the kettlebell goes over the shoulder and around to the back of the head. Be sure to keep your glutes clenched and your abs tight. Be sure, also, to keep your lower back flat. Bring the kettlebell over the other shoulder and back to the upside down goblet position at the front of your body.

Now change direction as you repeat the movement around the head and back to your chest. Your base position is both elbows tucked in at the chest. As you move you untuck one and then the other to facilitate the rotational movement. You should keep the path of the exercise comparable to a halo above the head. Try to keep the kettlebell close to the head throughout the movement. Don't allow your head to move throughout the exercise – keep it looking straight ahead. It helps to pick a spot on the wall in front of you and to keep your eyes focused on it throughout the movement. If you have to look down and drop the head then the kettlebell is too heavy. Lighten the load to allow proper technique.

Kettlebell Exercise No.2: Kettlebell Deadlift

The deadlift is a foundational exercise for developing strength in the posterior chain, including the muscles of the lower back, glutes and hamstrings. The kettlebell version also improves hip increasing technique, allowing for better performance on such exercises as snatches, cleans and swings.

Place the kettlebell on the floor between your legs and just in front of you. With your feet shoulder width apart, sit back with your hips, allowing yourself to go down until you can reach the handles. Keep your chest up throughout the movement. Now grab the handle with both hands and return to a standing position by pushing your heels into the ground. The power for the lift will come from your glutes, which should be squeezed tight, and your lower back (erector spine).

Next, repeat the descent by pushing the hips and gently lowering until the kettlebell just kisses the ground. It is important to keep the center of gravity aligned over your base while doing this movement. In addition, you should be creasing your body at the hips, rather than bending at the waist. Your lower back should be slightly arched throughout the movement. To target the hamstrings more, keep your legs straight throughout the movement. To place more emphasis on the glutes, bend your legs slightly on the descent. Keep your elbows back and chest up throughout the movement.

A variation on this movement is a double kettlebell deadlift, grabbing the kettlebells in a grocery bag type lift.

Kettlebell Exercise No.3: Two Handed Kettlebell Swing

The kettlebell swing is a classic kettlebell power developer. In order to perfect the technique follow a two-step process as outlined below:

Step One: With feet shoulder width apart, place the kettlebell between your toes. As in the deadlift, thrust you hips back to go down to the kettlebell (imagine that you are trying to close a car door with your butt). Keep your head up, ensuring that your shoulders don't get ahead of your knees. Grab the kettlebell with a two handed overhand grip. Rise up to a standing position quickly, popping your hips as you come up. Do this five times in rapid succession.

Step Two: Place the kettlebell back further so that the handle is in line with your heels. Repeat the movement that you have just performed. You will notice that, this time, there is a small pendulum effect at the top of the movement. Now try to drive the kettlebell back between your legs as you go down, so that it goes down, under your butt. On the ascent, pop the weight up to just below shoulder level. Be sure that you are not lifting with your arms or shoulders – the power must originate from the hips. This is one exercise where a pendulum like swing is desired. The use of momentum in this way reduces the strain on the lower back and grip while allowing for greater work capacity.

Kettlebell Exercise No.4: One Arm Clean

The one arm clean is a great intermediary movement between swing and pressing exercises. As you become proficient at this movement, you should develop a rhythmic motion, which flows from one rep into the next.

It's important that you maintain a loose grip on the kettlebell during this movement. This will prevent the bell from banging on your forearm as you perform the exercise. Begin with a slightly wider than shoulder width stance and the kettlebell sitting between your legs. Thrust your hips back, with lower back arched slightly, to come down and grip the kettlebell, with and over-hand grip, your thumb pointed behind you. Your non-working hand should be out to the side, with the fist closed. Maintain a good back posture with your head up.

Inhale as you clean the kettlebell to shoulder level. As you rise up, the kettlebell should swivel in your hand into a lock position. When you lock out at the top position, your glutes, quads and hamstrings should all be tight. As you rise, the kettlebell should move vertically up your body. At the top position, allow the kettlebell to rest on your chest and forearm in what is known as the rack position. The kettlebell should now be sitting in the triangle that is formed by the elbow, forearm and chest.

A common problem with this movement is uncomfortable banging of the kettlebell on the forearm. This occurs because you are gripping the handle too tight. Loosen the grip, allowing the fingers to go as deeply into the handle as possible as the kettlebell comes up to chest level.

Kettlebell Exercise No.5: Single Press

Begin with the kettlebell in the top position of the One Arm Clean (the rack position). Your elbow should be tucked into your stomach and your wrist and arm should be in a straight line. Put your non - working arm out to the side for stability. Drive the kettlebell up in a straight line until your elbow is completely locked out in the top position. Your hand should be positioned such that your thumb is pointing directly back behind you. Make sure that you are pushing with the whole body, as opposed to just the shoulders. The movement needs to include the flaring of the lats and the compression and extension of the spine.

Lower the kettlebell by moving your body slightly back to allow the kettlebell to return to the rack position. The up-down movement needs to be fluid, without any jerking movements.

Breathing should follow a four-stage pattern as follows:

(1)   Breath in deeply while holding the kettlebell in the rack position

(2)   Breath out just prior to the overhead push

(3)   Inhale as you drive up

(4)   Exhale as you lock out in the top position

Kettlebell Exercise No.6: Snatch

The kettlebell snatch is built off the kettlebell swing, so make sure that your form is on point for the swing before moving to this exercise. With feet shoulder width apart, place the kettlebell between your toes. Thrust you hips back to go down to the kettlebell. Keep your head up, ensuring that your shoulders don't get ahead of your knees. Grab the kettlebell with a one handed overhand grip. Rise up to a standing position quickly, popping your hips as you come up. Make sure to keep your shins vertical throughout the movement.

Get a good pendulum motion going with several swings, with the hips initiating the movement, and the arms simply doing the guiding. Everything should be locked out in the top position. After about five swings, take the kettlebell all the way up until it is locked out overhead. As you go up, the kettlebell will swivel over your hand until, in the lockout position, it is resting against the back of your lower arm. In the top position your palm should be open. Re-grip on the way down. If you are doing high reps, hold the top position for a second or two in order to catch your breath. Alternate arms after every five overhead snatches.

Kettlebell Exercise No.7: Goblet Squat

The Kettlebell Goblet Squat is a fantastic movement for opening up the hips, and building power in the lower body. With a slightly wider than shoulder width grip, grab the kettlebell by the horns and hold it at chest level. Keep your elbows in as you descend into a squat. Actively pull yourself down, with your glutes and hips going out and back. Don't go back too far, however, because you want to stay as upright as possible. Go straight down into a full squat. The elbows should come down and rest inside your knees and against your inner thighs in the bottom squat position. This will prevent your knees from collapsing in. The knees will come forward slightly, but should not go inwards. Thrust your chest out and look up from this position. They should, in fact, track your toes at all times. In this bottom position, shift the knees from side to side, using your elbows to pry your thighs apart. Push your tailbone down and your head up.

Now take a deep breath, exhale and drive straight back up to the starting position.

Kettlebell Exercise No.8 Windmill

The Windmill is a very effective movement for the hamstrings, glutes, lower back and shoulders. It also targets the core, while making your stronger and more stable in the overhead position. This movement is also a great way to enhance your overall flexibility.

Start in the rack position with your feet shoulder width apart. Power the kettlebell up to a locked out overhead position. Angle your feet at a forty-five degree angle to the arm which is holding the kettlebell. Shift about 95 percent of your weight to the inside leg that is bearing the weight. Now kick the kettlebell side hip out, while you lower to take your non-kettlebell arm down towards the toe on the same side. Keep the overhead arm locked out as you descend. Look up throughout the movement, using your leg as a guide to track your arm down towards the toe.

It is optional as to whether you lock out the front leg. However, the back leg must stay locked out through the entire movement. Do not shift the weight to the front leg during the downward part of the movement. Rather keep your weight on the rear leg by pushing the rear hip up and back. Your shoulder will rotate as you thrust out your hip and lower your upper body to the toe.

Kettlebell Exercise No.9: High Pull

The Kettlebell High Pull is a whole body movement that builds power and functional strength that will make you more explosive for such sports as sprinting, basketball, boxing and karate.

With feet shoulder width apart, place the kettlebell between your toes. Thrust you hips back to go down to the kettlebell. Keep your head up, ensuring that your shoulders don't get ahead of your knees. Grab the kettlebell with a two handed overhand grip at the top of the horns so that your thumbs are touching. Make sure that your shoulders are in front of the weight. Begin the pull by pushing down through your feet and driving your hips up and forward. Keep your arms extended through this first part of the pull. Use the force of the leg drive to extend your body upward. Lift the kettlebell to chest level. Let your momentum carry you up on to your toes, then squat down to the start position. In the top position, your elbows should be elevated above the weight.

Kettlebell Exercise No.10: Turkish Get Up

The Turkish Get Up is a phenomenal total body exercise. It is great for cardiovascular conditioning as well for building functional strength and power. Start by lying on the floor, on your back with your knees bent. The kettlebell should be on the floor to your right. Place your right hand fully into the kettlebell handle and pull the weight to your chest. Now, with both shoulder blades on the floor, raise your right arm straight up so that the kettlebell is directly above your chest. The right knee should be bent so that the right foot is flat on the floor. Your left arm should be flat on the floor at a forty five degree angle.

From the start position, rise up onto your left elbow, keeping the right arm locked. From there, come up further so that you are supporting your body with just your left hand and your right foot. Your left leg should be straight and a few inches off the floor. Now move your butt and left leg back behind you to rest your left knee on the ground. You can now rise up to the lunge position, with your left hand off the floor and the points of contact now being your right foot and left shin. The kettlebell is still locked overhead.

Pushing off the back leg rise to a standing position. Keep your focus up on the kettlebell the whole time. Now reverse the exact motion to return to the start position.

Kettlebell Exercise No.11: Russian Twist

The Russian Twist is a very good movement to develop phenomenal core strength, while shaping and defining the obliques. Sit upright on the floor with a kettlebell alongside you, then lean back a little so that your abs are tensed to keep you up. Bend your knees and, keeping your legs together; elevate the feet to about six inches off the floor. Grab hold of the kettlebell with an overhand grip towards the top of the horns. Starting with the kettlebell sitting at your waist, rotate to the right to bring the weight to the floor. Once it touches, immediately rotate to the other side and touch the floor there. Repeat back and forth, making sure that you touch the kettlebell to the floor each time. You need to also ensure that your feet are off the ground throughout the entire motion.

Kettlebell Exercise No.12: Two Arm Kettlebell Row

This is a great exercise for developing functional strength in the muscle of the upper back, arms and shoulders. Start by placing a pair of kettlebells on the floor wide enough apart that you can step through them. Keeping your heels on the floor, bend down to grab the kettlebell handles. Let your hips track back and maintain an arch in your lower back as you go down. From there, soften your knees and push your glutes into the air. This will ensure a flat back position. Now breathe in as you pull your arms up to your chest. Keep the tension in the back muscles and the muscles of the upper arm. Control the kettlebells as you return them to the start position. Don't let the shoulders roll forward.

Kettlebell Exercise No.13: Lunge Clean / Lunge Press

This is a fluid movement that allows you to get a great power / cardio combination workout. It is beneficial for your heart and lungs and is a tremendous fat burner. Start by holding a kettlebell at your right side, with feet shoulder width apart. Now lunge forward with your right leg. As you come out of the lunge, clean the kettlebell to your right shoulder. Now continue moving forward by lunging with your left foot. As you come out of this lunge, press the kettlebell overhead. Continue this lunge-clean-lunge-process for the required time allotment.

Chapter 4: The Essentials Techniques

I thought it would be good to briefly go over some of the basics, when it comes to lifting weights. If you are familiar with the basics, then you can skip this section, or you can scan it over quickly if you need a refresher.

These are the essential things you should do when you perform your kettlebell workouts. These things will help you avoid injury and get more out of your workouts.

Time Under Tension is important for muscle growth – Time under tension (TUT) is one mistake I see all the time. Many beginners don't realize the importance of TUT and they wonder why their results suck. Time under tension is basically what it sounds like, the amount of time your muscle are under tension while performing an exercise. Usually the more tension time you have, the more you will stimulate muscle growth.

I think a lot of beginners see professional bodybuilder working out and they are performing their reps really fast. But I think that they miss the point of, professional bodybuilder take steroids and they can get away with performing fast reps because their gains are aided artificially. So for the most of us performing slow repetitions will give you the biggest bang for your buck.

Usually but not all the time considering the different exercises you will be performing, but for most of the time I suggest you perform 5 seconds for each motion you are moving the weight. So for example, when you are performing a squat, go down 5 seconds and raise for 5 seconds.

There's a good article you can read from SimplyShredded.com that go more into detail about TUT in the resource section.

Breathe correctly – Out of all the things I recommend you make sure you do is breathe correctly. If you aren't breathing correctly, or not breathing at all while you are working out, you WILL serious damage your body in one way or another. You can easily pull something if you are holding your breath while you perform exercises with heavy weight. That is why you must always breath and do it the right way to avoid some serious issues down the road.

In order to breathe correctly you must do two simple things. To make it less confusing let me again use the squat example I used earlier. When you are lowering your body while performing the squat you want to breathe in. When you are brining your body up we want to breathe out. The same concept applies to every exercise, like for example when you are performing a bench press. As you lower the weight you breathe in and when you are pushing the weight up, you should breathe out.

Medium Grip — This one is especially important for using kettlebells. Depending on the exercise you are performing you will generally want to have a medium grip while holding the kettlebell. You want to make sure that you are not holding it too tight so like it's a death grip, but you also don't want to hold the kettlebell too loose so that it falls out of your hand.

As you learn some exercises like the kettlebell snatch you will learn why this is important to know. Basically some exercises involve you moving your grip on the kettlebell to perform the exercise. So just remember to most of the time keep your grip in the middle.

Keep your head up looking in front up you – This point and the next point are two of the most crucial things you need to do in order to prevent injury while you workout. It is best to always to keep your head straight with your eyes looking in front of you, although some kettlebell exercises require you to look at the kettlebell while performing the exercise. But for the most part you want to keep your head up, especially if you are performing an exercise where you are standing or are bent over. This will help avoid injury in your neck and upper body.

Keep You back Straight – The other thing that is really important if you want to prevent injuries while working out is to keep you back straight. This is recommend for practically any type of exercise you may be doing. Picture a line being drawn down you back as you are exercising. If you don't follow this you will experience some painful injuries that you may never be able to correct in the future. You can easily pull a muscle if you don't follow this point.

Chapter 5: Advantages Of Physical Exercise Using Kettlebells

Kettlebell workouts provide significant advantage to people, particularly exercisers and sports practitioners. Some of the surefire benefits include:

Enhanced physiologic conditions and dexterity

Improved posture and better alignment. A lot of the exercises affect the core stability muscles effectively.

This training is effective and no time is wasted in doing the movements. The exerciser works out a number of areas in physical fitness in one training session, which includes strength, cardio, balance, power, endurance, and stability.

Every movement with the weight affects how the different parts of the body are worked up, which facilitates increased density of the bones. It helps maintain the strength and power of the body for activities of daily living.

The exerciser or athlete becomes more capable when performing other forms of exercise.

Helps to develop the size of skeletal muscles, greater strength, and staying power. These are highly beneficial for different types of sports.

This workout can safeguard athletes from getting injured. A lot of accidents can occur when a person moves in high-speed and then immediately discontinues, as a technique in the training. Kettlebell exercises actually work the body in this aspect, which can lead to a more improved body in terms of health and power while doing sports activities.

Less risk for injury when using the appropriate weights with excellent and precise movements.

Kettlebell training is very simple. The movements are not complicated to perform. Every physical activity is clear-cut and does not require bulky and complicated machines.

Individuals who are interested to engage in kettlebell training can attend or join a class of exercisers. They can also train under supervision from a reliable and experienced trainer. This is necessary to have a comprehensive rundown of the workouts. A lot of the swing actions may not be familiar so an expert can provide assistance when it comes to particular movements and in deciding the weights required for the different types of exercises.

Chapter 6: The Numerous Benefits

Of Kettlebell Training

There are numerous exercise tools and equipment out there. They are all quite useful and provide their own unique benefits. I will never tell you that a piece of workout equipment is wrong for you. Especially if you've experienced positive results. I will, however, suggest that a particular type of equipment is more beneficial and practical if it can provide the functions of multiple tools at the same time. A Swiss army knife is certainly more useful than a regular pocket knife. Whatever your fitness goals may be, the kettlebell can help you reach them. The most critical part, as we mentioned in chapter 2, is making sure to get the one that fits you best.

Kettlebell exercises bring together a combination of cardiovascular and strength training, the two major sectors that result in muscle gain, fat reduction, weight loss, and overall well-being. With the intensity of the workouts and variety of body parts targeted with each, you will notice extreme fat burn and muscle buildup in no time. I noticed it in a major way myself, and I have been working out for as long as I can remember.

If my story is not enticing enough for you, consider a few others. A former top fighter from K1, Bob Sapp, has praised the kettlebell for enhancing his cardio with his training. Former UFC welterweight champion BJ Penn uses kettlebell training to increase his muscular endurance. Both Bob Sapp and BJ Penn have had massive success against top-level fighters in their respective organizations. Hollywood actor Ed O'Neil, who is a staunch practitioner of Brazilian Jiu-Jitsu, is also a huge fan of kettlebell training. It has been getting more and more praise from fitness fanatics around the world and is taking off like never before.

This may be one of the reasons why people think it's a fad. When celebrities jump on various trends, it can be hard to tell if they are serious, or just want the publicity. As I mentioned before, the kettlebell has been around for centuries, and just started getting worldwide notoriety during the 2000s. It is not a fad as numerous practitioners around the world sing its praises. This includes me. The kettlebell has done wonders for me, well beyond what I experienced at the height of my competitive days. This piece of equipment can do wonders for you too.

CARDIOVASCULAR AND STRENGTH TRAINING

There are many workouts that provide amazing cardiovascular and strength training. However, very few offer them together. Common kettlebell routines, like swings, snatches, cleans, and jerks, workout your whole body as one unit. Essentially, you are working out a wide array of muscles and body parts within a couple of minutes and the routines are intense. You are going to feel them in a big way and probably put in more effort than you ever have before.

Ballistic kettlebell exercises like high rep snatches can make sprinting look like a walk in the park. Sprinting, in reality, is anything but that. Rep snatches also target many more muscle groups than sprinting, and will significantly build strength in the lower back, shoulders, and hips. With the various high-intensity exercises that one can do with a kettlebell, each muscle in the body will receive a workout like never before.

Recent studies have shown that the swing can burn up to 20 calories per minute. That's 400 calories in a 20 minutes workout when done properly. That's a very high level of calorie burn. Also, with the high intensity, you have the afterburn. This means you are still burning calories at a high rate even after the workout is complete. You would have to run for a much longer period with at least a 6-minute mile pace to even come close to these results.

Kettlebell workouts are much more appealing for men than things like step aerobics or spinning classes. Most men are very self-conscious about these exercises and feel like idiots when they do them. This causes them to not get the level of workout they desperately want and need. I am not knocking these exercises. I think they are great. I am just stating a reality here. Men feel better about themselves doing ballistic kettlebell workouts over something like Zumba. You can take ballistic kettlebell exercises up a notch by combining them with activities like jump roping or jogging.

Using the kettlebell improves our functional strength also. This is because it mimics our muscles' movements and functions as they occur in their natural state. Our muscles do not work in isolation. They perform in conjunction with one another to avoid excess muscle strain, prevent injuries, perform more efficiently, and build strength. As an example, our leg muscles are not working alone when we are walking. The work is distributed across the body, so everything is working together efficiently. Kettlebell training follows this same concept. When we learn to use our muscles together with various training methods, this carries over to the functionality of our everyday lives. Through proper functional training methods, you will reduce the risk of injury in your everyday lives, while also increasing your strength, agility, flexibility, and balance.

Kettlebells also increase your core strength and stability. Since many kettlebell exercises are ballistic training, they center around explosive movements by maximizing acceleration and minimizing deceleration. Abdominal muscles are heavily stimulated with these movements due to their high intensity and core contraction. Remember to always coordinate your core contractions with proper breathing because of the high intensity. You will feel your core strength increase tremendously, even more so than with targeted exercises like crunches or leg raises. Plus, kettlebell exercises put less strain on your back and don't require you to lay on the floor as crunches do. Of course, there are specific crunch exercise routines as well that we will go over.

Movements with the kettlebell workout your core from multiple directions because they are multiplanar. The unilateral movements also offer major strength and stability to your core. You will notice a major increase in your core strength after performing just a few workouts. As you begin actively performing the different workouts at all levels, you will immediately understand what core engagement means.

Many athletes train with the kettlebell for this very reason. They need extreme core power to move through their competition, change directions in an instant, and handle major loads from either side. The training done with kettlebells gives a person the physical capabilities to handle these types of pressures. Mike Tyson was one of the most ferocious heavyweight boxers in history. He would decimate his opponents and run right over them, seemingly with ease.

The interesting thing is, Tyson was not a big guy. At least, not compared to some of the heavyweight giants out there. So, how was he able to push people around the ring and not get pushed around back? Because of his amazing core strength. He was rock solid in this area, which meant he could move forward, side-to-side, and make last-minute adjustments when needed. He could easily absorb punches that did land on his body for this very reason. If the kettlebell can give professional level athletes the core strength they need, imagine what it can do for your everyday needs. This area of strength is essential to becoming a fitness beast.

One aspect of strength training that is often ignored is grip strength. This is kind of ironic since one of the main times two men test strength is when they are shaking hands. One would think that this is a common concern in any workout routine. Nonetheless, a poor grip will give you major disadvantages in a number of exercises. A strong grip will lead to being able to lift more weights. Plus, the stronger your grip, the larger and stronger your forearms will become. The kettlebell has immensely improved the grip strength for many people who have used it.

There are two factors at play here. First of all, the handle is larger than a regular dumbbell, so your grip will automatically be more stressed. Second, the nature of kettlebell exercises will put more unnatural stress on your hands and forearms, causing more engagement of the muscles in the area. For example, the swing requires you to hold the kettlebell for an extended period of time, while having to counter a constantly changing center of gravity. All of this will lead to a tighter grip. After some time working out with a kettlebell, go up and shake your friends' hands. They will be quite impressed. Don't grip too hard. You don't want to hurt them.

Working out with the kettlebell will immensely improve your strength and conditioning. Not only will you feel better during your workout routines, but also while living your life day-to-day. You will have far more energy while running errands. That long staircase won't seem as daunting. Whatever hobbies you enjoy, it will be easier to do them because you will have more stamina. You won't feel as tired at work, which means you will be more productive. Exercising with the kettlebell can start improving your quality of life as a whole.

BALANCE AND POWER

When you are running on a treadmill or using most types of machines, you are moving on a predetermined path. There are not many directions you can go while running on a treadmill. Even if you get creative, you are still quite limited in how many muscles you can engage. When using a kettlebell, you have more diversity in your movements. For this, you need to double down on your strength of the stabilizer muscle with every moment. When you combine this strength increase of the stabilizer muscles with the core strength we discussed earlier, your balance will become tremendous. You are basically building stability using instability.

Kettlebell training will also help your balance by teaching you to contend with a constant change in the center of gravity. With the various stances and positions you take during each workout, the center of gravity of the kettlebell lays at least 6-8 inches outside of your grip. This causes you to contend with a force that challenges your balance, which is something you will encounter on a regular basis with your activities of daily living.

As an offshoot of balance, kettlebell usage is excellent for improving posture. A large number of exercises target the entire backside. This includes your upper, middle, and lower back, plus your glutes, hamstrings, and traps. All of the muscles in these areas will become extremely powerful, which will result in improved posture. Strengthening your neck muscles, core, hips, and shoulders will contribute to this benefit as well.

We spoke earlier about strength and how kettlebell exercises significantly improve your strength endurance in all areas of the body. The kettlebell also increases your power output. This is a little bit different than strength. Strength refers to your ability to produce force over an extended period of time. Power adds another element to it as it relates more to the explosiveness of the movement involved. Power is basically the body's ability to generate as much force as possible, as quickly as possible. Kettlebell training does this by making you perform fast and explosive movements over and over again. Power is what ultimately wins in most athletic competitions.

Regarding power, let's go back to our friend Mike Tyson again. There is no doubt Mike is a strong guy. If you match him up against someone from a strongman competition and they have a pushing contest, the strongman will probably win. He will be able to generate more force over a stronger period of time. However, if the two had a punching contest, Mike Tyson would probably win because he can generate a higher force more quickly, meaning he has more explosiveness. Essentially, the strongman is stronger, but Tyson is more powerful.

PAIN BE GONE

A major benefit to kettlebell workouts is the extreme reduction in pain throughout the body. Many people suffer from lower back pain due to weak glute muscles, which make up the buttocks area. These muscles are the largest in the body and are responsible for almost all movement. When they are weak, they do not carry their necessary load, so much of the work falls onto the lower back muscles. These muscles are not designed to carry the same amount of weight as the glutes. Over time, the lower back begins feeling the strain and chronic pain becomes a major issue. This can lead to major injuries down the line that become debilitating. As we strengthen our glute muscles with continuous kettlebell exercises, we give them the ability to start carrying their share. This will significantly reduce the workload on the back and effectively reduce lower back pain.

Major pain due to arthritis can also be prevented as kettlebell exercises improve and maintain joint health. The various workouts require deliberate control during movements, which strengthens the muscles that support your joints. In addition, the elasticity that develops in the ligaments and tendons will increase mobility and help prevent major injuries like strains, sprains, and tears. You will become much more resilient overall.

CONVENIENCE AND OTHER ADVANTAGES

We have discussed numerous advantages already to the kettlebell. One of the most appealing things about them is the convenience. You can work out regularly and intensely without ever having to walk into a gym. If it's raining, snowing, or hailing, you have this piece of equipment at your disposal. Just walk to your closet, or wherever you may keep it, and start your routine with various reps. Within 20 minutes of high-intensity training, you will be drenched in sweat, and feel a great sense of accomplishment because you put in a great workout.

If you don't want to want to stay at home and workout, you certainly don't have to. The kettlebell is compact and can be carried to many different locations. If you feel like you need some fresh air, take it with you to your local park and do some basic routines there. You can even keep one at work and do some reps during your breaks. Just make sure to not sweat too much while at the office. It's not a very good look for a business environment. If you do like working out at the gym, then chances are they will have kettlebells there too.

The main point is that you can use this diverse piece of equipment almost anywhere. It is very convenient and will provide a great workout at the drop of a hat. No other exercise equipment is required. Of course, you can use others if you choose. As we mentioned before, there are many exercises that can complement the kettlebell, but very few that can replace it. One fact about the kettlebell workouts that I have not pointed out yet is that they are extremely fun to do. You'll probably not miss doing anything else. I will say that it is great only having to worry about having kettlebells in the house, which can easily be stored in a closet or in the corner, versus a treadmill or elliptical, which takes up half of a living room.

There are numerous other advantages that the kettlebell provides. The workouts can be used for active recovery. Adequate recovery is extremely important for athletes or active individuals in general. Unfortunately, sitting on the couch and eating junk food is not a beneficial recovery process. You will come back sluggish and in worse shape than before. If you try to jump back into an exercise schedule, you will basically be starting over. The key is to maintain conditioning. This can be done with some light training exercises to get some blood into the worked muscles. This will speed up the recovery process immensely and keep you in shape in between high-intensity workouts.

One way to use the kettlebell effectively for recovery is to follow some of the regimens of Jeff Martone, who is the Physical Training and Combative

Coordinator at the Direct Action Resource Center. Mr. Martone knows a lot about conditioning. Through many of his videos, he goes over several kettlebell drills where you pass the kettlebell from hand to hand in mid-air. In addition to maintaining blood flow in the muscles, these exercises also improve hand-eye coordination, grip strength, and the ability to absorb shock. The routines also test your brain, so not only will you be physically tired, but mentally drained as well.

We have mentioned this before but will reiterate again, that kettlebell exercises are an extreme time saver. If you could choose between a workout that is 20 minutes versus 60 minutes, and both burn the same number of calories, which one would you pick? With workouts, quality means more than quantity. If you have been to the gym enough times, you have probably noticed the varying level of effort being put in by different individuals. One person is grinding and pushing themselves to the max, while another is barely going through the motions. The first individual will get significantly better results, no matter how long each person works out. To get great outcomes, you have to be more than only present. you have to be fully engaged.

With the kettlebell, when used properly, you will get amazing results. You will burn the same number of calories in 20 minutes than you would with about an hour of running or biking. This is also considering how hard you push yourself while doing these exercises. Imagine grabbing a kettlebell in the morning, afternoon, or evening, and doing some intense routines for 20 minutes and feeling so much better afterward. You didn't have to leave your house, fix your hair, or really look presentable in any way. You simply started and were done before you knew it. This is not a dream, but a reality. 20 minutes a day, for at least a few days a week is definitely doable, I don't care how busy you are. The fact that you don't have to leave your home is an added bonus. The "I don't have time" excuse is non-existent here. You have time, you just have to use it.

The kettlebell is an amazing product and my only regret is not finding it sooner in life. With all of the great benefits, it is hard to not consider it a great investment. For those of you worried about the cost, compare it to a monthly gym membership or the various exercise equipment you'll need to cover all areas of the body. Furthermore, consider other expenses you can cut out or reduce that will make this investment easier to afford. I am not a financial planner, so I don't want to get too far into this. One thing to remember is, once you get a good kettlebell or two, they will last you a very long time. The sooner you can get one, the better. Go out there and own it.

Chapter 7: Nutrition

It would be unwise to assert that nutrition is a one size fits all kind of gambit. Some rules must be followed to ensure your body transformation. One should ensure they are getting enough proteins without exceeding on calories. Macronutrients are vital. For a fit and healthy body your body requires the right nutrients and in the correct proportions. Most people take the wrong route when they decide to diet, they do this by lowering their caloric intake and this involves cutting down on carbohydrates. This would be correct if the carbs come from junk food cakes excess bread and candy. When the body is exposed to drastic changes in the diet it adapts to chemical processes as it aims to safeguard its glucose stores.

Carbohydrates are the main source of energy that fuels the functioning of the muscles. Carbohydrates are broken down in the body into smaller elements that the body can utilize. They are stored in form of glycogen in muscles fat and liver and can be accessed when the need arises. For this reason, sudden drastic changes can be counter-productive because if the body noticed a drop in supply it would adjust by protecting the already available. This means metabolism slows down to preserve energy. During extreme carbohydrate shortage when glycogen stores are depleted the body metabolizes its own protein to provide energy. This leads to the breakdown of muscle skin hair and bones making the body have that appearance of a starving person.

Apart from providing energy needed for cellular function and growth carbohydrates also perform the following functions within the body;

Regulate blood sugar levels

Help in calcium absorption

Provide nutrients for probiotics in the intestinal tract

Assist in regulating blood pressure and cholesterol levels

Fuel the CNS and the brain

In maintaining a healthy diet selecting protein, vitamins and minerals from natural sources while at the same time avoiding processed foods serves as the most important step towards maintaining health.

An appropriate diet consists of the following elements;

Proteins from fish lean meats and nuts

Vegetables and fruits

While grains and alternate carbs such as barley corn meal and beans

Dairy including milk cheese and yoghurt

Healthy fats and oils

Limited amounts of refined grains eg potatoes and white rice

Minimal amounts of other items like salt sugar and alcohol.

There is no ideal diet plan that will fit the needs of every individual and when planning your diet common sense and some little knowledge regarding ingredients and nutrients is important. Always consider the following

Pay attention to the size of the portions. One should eat better and not more

Select a wide range of food sources that will help cover your nutritional needs

At each meal the choice of carbs to be taken should be carefully chosen

Always choose foods that are of higher quality. Less processed, more natural

Always take breakfast, and healthy snacks in midmorning and mid afternoon

Ensure you include a small portion of lean protein

Avoid caffeine and drink green tea

Never underestimate the need to stay hydrated. Drink plenty of water.

Add spices and herbs to help aid digestion

When working out itys important to keep the body hydrated to replace the fluids lost through sweats. Intense workouts can create a huge water demand of even 2-3 gallons of water daily. Water is important for the following functions

Provides the fluid portion of blood that transports oxygen and other nutrients.

Gets rid of toxins and cellular waste products from the body in solution form

Helps in thermoregulation

Helps improve digestion

Chapter 8: Kettlebell Deadlift

This is another classic compound movement. The deadlift is the king of all leg exercises and the kettlebell deadlift is no different.

Muscles Targeted: Legs, Arms, Back, Core, and Glutes

Method:

Stand with your legs a little closer together then your shoulder width and place the kettlebell between your feet. Squat down and place both hands on the kettlebell so that your knuckles are pointing in front of you. Remember to keep your back flat, and bend with your knees and hips. Engage your core and glutes and tighten your arms while keeping them extended. Stand up, driving your hips upwards. Pause at the top and squeeze before reversing the movement and placing the kettlebell back in it's starting position.

Video:

https://www.youtube.com/watch?v=B0y spkANWVY

Top Tips:

- Keep your back flat!

- Keep your neck in a neutral position and look ahead.

- Don't overextend and roll backwards.

- Aim for a smooth rep not necessarily a fast one.

Two arm kettlebell row

The two-arm kettlebell row is great for working the back and shoulders.

It relies on a straight back and tight core.

Muscles Targeted: Arms, Back and Shoulders

Method:

Stand a shoulder width apart and place a kettlebell in front of each foot. Bend at the knees slightly, keeping your black flat and your neck in a neutral position. Grab both the kettlebells with your knuckles facing each other. Pull the kettlebells up towards your stomach. You shouldn't aim to stand up, move your knees or back. This is a row so the movement should be as if on a rowing machine, with your elbows moving backwards. Aim to keep the movement in both arms equal with each other. The movement should be fluid. Keep your elbows close to your body. At the top of the rep tense your core and keep everything tight, then slowly drop the weights in a controlled motion back towards the starting position. Repeat.

Video: https://www.youtube.com/watch?v=03KANlPwWWQ

Top tips:

- Don't crane your neck upwards, aim to keep your neck in a neutral position.

- Visualize the movement while doing it. It should be fluid and piston like.

Kettlebell Russian twist

The Russian twist is one of the most effective exercises for building strong defined abs and building core strength.

Muscles Targeted: Abs, Obliques

Method:

Sit with your legs bent at the knees and your feet flat on the floor. The starting position is similar to that of a crunch, but with your legs about a hip distance apart. Pick up the Kettlebell with both hands and bring it up to your chest. Lean back a little so you are at a 45-degree angle. Twist your torso from left to right. The movement should start at the waist and be controlled at all times. Do not swing the weight from side to side, but rather imagine you are picking up the weight from your left side and bring it over your body to place on the other side, before repeating the opposite way round.

Video:
https://www.youtube.com/watch?v=vcw9 0-Cc1LY

Top Tips:

- Try to keep this movement as controlled as possible, don't erratically swing the weight from side to side.

- Keep your core tight the whole time and maintain that 45-degree angle.

Kettlebell Windmill

The Kettlebell windmill is a great exercise for hitting upper body.

Muscles Targeted: Shoulders, Hips, Back, Abs and Obliques

Method:

Hold the kettlebell handle in one hand and angle your feet away from the arm holding the kettlebell. Place the majority of your weight on whichever foot is on the side with the kettlebell. Raise the kettlebell over your head and lock your arm in place. Look up at the kettlebell, this will keep your shoulders aligned. Move your weight onto the other leg and bend forward at the waist. All the time you should keep the weight above your head with your arm locked. The hand without the kettlebell should point towards the ground, stretch down as far as you can go and hold the position for a second. Slowly reverse the potion and lift back up. Keep the movement slow and controlled at all times.

Video:
https://www.youtube.com/watch?v=yKik0YFE370

Top Tips:

- Maintain eye contact with the kettlebell at all times to keep your shoulders aligned.

- Don't rush the movement. Focus on form and control.

Chapter 9: Lower Body Kettlebell Exercises

Kettlebell Squat (Thighs)

– Hold the kettlebell at chest level using both hands, with your elbows tucked in and your hands close to your torso.

– Your feet must be a bit wider than shoulder-width apart and your toes must be pointed slightly towards the outside.

– Tighten your abs and keep your lower back straight. This is the beginning position of the exercise.

– Gradually bend your knees, bring your hips back, and lower your legs to the point that your thighs are a little bit below parallel with the ground. As you do this, inhale.

– Return to the original or beginning position by pushing your hips through and pressing through your heels. As you do this, exhale. This constitutes 1 rep.

– Do 8 to 12 reps per set.

One-Legged   Kettlebell   Deadlift
(Hamstrings)

– Start by standing on one leg with a kettlebell in one hand, the hand on the same side of the leg on which you're standing on.

– With your standing leg's knee bent slightly, do a stiff-legged deadlift by extending the other leg towards your back, as you bend at the hips. Extending the other leg will help you balance your body during the movement.

– Continue bringing the down the kettlebell until your upper body's just about parallel to the floor.

– Reverse the movement and return to the starting position to complete 1 rep.

– Do 8 to 12 reps per set.

Kettlebell Bulgarian Split Squat (Thighs and Glutes)

– With one foot placed on top of a box or bench behind you, hold a kettle bell in each hand.

– Resting your bodyweight on the heel of the front leg and chest forward, lower your body until the knee of the leg that's up on the box or platform behind you touches the ground. Make sure that the knee of the front leg never goes beyond the toes to minimize risks for knee injuries.

– Return to the original position to complete 1 rep. Do 8-12 reps per set per leg.

Chapter 10: Cross Training

Aside from using kettlebells with the CrossFit program, you could also use it while practicing and preparing for another sport. CrossFit is often used by professionals who rely on their fitness to do their jobs properly. Many firemen, policemen and paramedics use it all over the country. You will benefit even more from this program if you join the sports that the CrossFit community around you plays.

By using cross training in your workout routines, you will expose your body to more movements that challenge every part of it. Focusing on only a few muscle groups all the time is inadequate if you want to develop overall fitness. People often feel out of shape when they are doing a new set of exercises or a new type of sports. A fitness buff who is used to working out his upper body may feel really out of shape when they are jogging. If you put a body builder in a running game like basketball, they often feel inadequate because of the lack of practice. They are not accustomed to the speed and the flexibility that the sport requires.

This is where cross training can help. By constantly looking for new sports and workout regimens to try, we are developing all the aspects of our fitness. We are also increasing our skill set not only in sports but also in the physical requirements of life.

How to start cross training

Train for two types of sports

You can handpick the workout moves suggested in this book to train for a sport. When studying a new sport, take note of the key movements that you need to practice and the muscles that you need to develop to be able to execute those movements effectively. You should then choose the kettlebell workouts of the day that target these movements.

Include flexibility and speed in your training

When cross training, you should never neglect the other aspects of fitness that most muscle-builders forget; flexibility and speed. Luckily, the workouts that improve these aspects of fitness can be done with minimal equipment.

Learn a new sport every year

Many people only focus on two or three types of sports or workout activities when they are cross train. Some of them however, get tired of the monotony of these sports. The monotony in training also adds to the rigidity of the joints decreasing flexibility and agility. To keep your body in shape and to keep challenging it, you should learn a new sport ever year. Some people who have mastered sport swimming for example, transfer to learning surfing or diving. Choose sports that are related to the current sports that you are practicing.

Chapter 11: Reasons For The Kettlebell Training

- Muscle Building

Exercises with the kettlebell usually train multiple muscles at the same time, i.e. they are functional and effective. For example, those who integrate the kettlebell swing into their training train not only their legs and buttocks but also their calves, back and ensure a good stabilization of the middle of the body. Although the tension of the entire body is needed, but primarily the legs, butt and back are addressed, which is very important for office stools and thus the perfect exercise for the multi-seated in the office.

- Fat loss

Through short but intensive training sessions, circulation, and metabolism are maximized. The result is an afterburn effect, which has a favorable impact on fat burning. Also, the Kettlebell Swing, for example, caused by the many mentioned muscles high energy consumption and also supports fat burning.

- Little Space

The training tool is small and does not take up much space. All exercises can be completed in the gym as well as easy at home. A kettlebell workout is perfect for your gym at home. But maybe you also want to go to the sun and carry your kettlebell into the park-like me.

- Short workouts = little time spent

A training session of 15-30 minutes is enough to burn about 300 calories, turn on the afterburning effect, and get your workout done. So it's a great addition to the full-time job.

- Everyday training

All the exercises you do with the kettlebell will benefit your everyday life. Why? The kettlebell permanently shifts its center of gravity during training, including a baby that moves in your arm and you react to it. Or your shopping bag which is never the same weight and also the stairs must be carried up. the more every day your exercises are, the more effective your training will be for you.

In everyday life, there is rarely only an isolated movement. The stretching to the glasses in the cupboard may look like a single-arm movement upwards, but still requires your calves to come on tiptoe, the torso to not fall over and to stretch the arm and grab a glass will activate all the muscles in the arm.

Chapter 12: Advanced Kettlebell Workouts.

Workout 3A - Darth Vader

"Impressive. Most impressive. Obi-Wan has taught you well. You have controlled your fear. Now, release your anger. Only your hatred can destroy me" - Darth Vader

Can't destroy you today, I'm too busy being awesome.

Time: About 10 minutes

Exercises: Two Handed Kettlebell Swing

If you feel any pain or discomfort end the workout immediately.

15 Seconds - 2 Handed Kettlebell Swings

15 Seconds - Rest

15 Seconds - 2 Handed Kettlebell Swings

15 Seconds - Rest

15 Seconds - 2 Handed Kettlebell Swings

15 Seconds - Rest

15 Seconds - 2 Handed Kettlebell Swings

15 Seconds - Rest

15 Seconds - 2 Handed Kettlebell Swings

15 Seconds - Rest

And so on until you have done 5 minutes of kettlebell swings. That will be 20 rounds of 15 seconds of swings and a 15 second rest. This is what is known as a HIIT workout (High Intensity Interval Training). This will undoubtedly get you breathing heavily and sweating. Due to the fat burning power of kettlebells paired with the fat burning power of HIIT workouts you will see a massive difference if you do this workout one or two times a week.

Workout 3B - The Superman

"You will give the people of Earth an ideal to strive towards. They will race behind you, they will stumble, they will fall. But in time, they will join you in the sun, Kal. In time, you will help them accomplish wonders. " - Jor-El

No need to go outside in your underwear do it from the comfort of your own home.

Time: About 10 minutes

Exercises: Two Handed Kettlebell Swing

If you feel any pain or discomfort end the workout immediately.

30 Seconds - 2 Handed Kettlebell Swings

30 Seconds - Rest

30 Seconds - 2 Handed Kettlebell Swings

30 Seconds - Rest

30 Seconds - 2 Handed Kettlebell Swings

30 Seconds - Rest

30 Seconds - 2 Handed Kettlebell Swings

30 Seconds - Rest

30 Seconds - 2 Handed Kettlebell Swings

30 Seconds - Rest

And so on until you have done 5 minutes of kettlebell swings. That will be 10 rounds of 30 seconds of swings and a 30 second rest. This workout will be significantly harder than the last one after about 6 rounds. You will feel like quitting but stay the course and keep going.

Workout 3C - Jon Snow

"You know nothing, Jon Snow." - Ygritte

He might not know nothing about most things but he knows that this workout is hard work.

Time: About 10 minutes

Exercises: Two Handed Kettlebell Swing

If you feel any pain or discomfort end the workout immediately.

60 Seconds - 2 Handed Kettlebell Swings

60 Seconds - Rest

60 Seconds - 2 Handed Kettlebell Swings

60 Seconds - Rest

60 Seconds - 2 Handed Kettlebell Swings

60 Seconds - Rest

60 Seconds - 2 Handed Kettlebell Swings

60 Seconds - Rest

60 Seconds - 2 Handed Kettlebell Swings

60 Seconds - Rest

And so on until you have done 5 minutes of kettlebell swings. That will be 5 rounds of 1 minute of swings and a 1 minute rest. This workout will be significantly harder than the last one after about 6 rounds. You arms will feel like lead weights by the halfway point of this workout.

The Iron Throne

"There is a savage beast in every man, and when you hand that man a sword or spear and send him forth to war, the beast stirs."

This is the brutal Kettlebell workout I have ever done. The Red Wedding has nothing on this!

Time: About 10 minutes

Exercises: Two Handed Kettlebell Swing, Two handed Kettlebell Squat

If you feel any pain or discomfort end the workout immediately.

60 Seconds - 2 Handed Kettlebell Swings

60 Seconds - Kettlebell Squat

60 Seconds - 2 Handed Kettlebell Swings

60 Seconds - Kettlebell Squat

60 Seconds - 2 Handed Kettlebell Swings

60 Seconds - Kettlebell Squat

60 Seconds - 2 Handed Kettlebell Swings

60 Seconds - Kettlebell Squat

60 Seconds - 2 Handed Kettlebell Swings

60 Seconds - Kettlebell Squat

And so on until you have done 5 minutes of kettlebell swings and kettlebell squats. That will be 5 rounds of 1 minute of swings and 1 minute of squats immediately after. This workout will mentally and physically break you. If you need a rest take one but try and go for as long as you can without needing it. You will need a long lie down after finishing. Congratulations you have made it to the hardest workout in the book.

Chapter 13: Targeting Your Chest

Kettlebell Swiss Ball Press

Great exercise for building your strength on multiple planes of motion and strengthening your core.

This move also teaches both sides of your body to work independently unlike the standard bench press.

As you are pressing the kettlebell aim to roll back and forward on the Swiss ball to hit different planes of motion.

Aim for 30 x reps, 15 per side for 3 x sets.

Lay back on the Swiss ball with a kettlebell either side of your feet.

Grip both kettlebells and curl them so the body of each kettlebell is resting on your biceps.

Press the kettlebell through to full extension of your arm.

Repeat alternating sides aiming to vary the ranges of motion.

Swiss-ball Pushup and Jackknife

Great for core and chest as makes the push-up more difficult, with the incline angle and the balancing aspect of the swissball

Try different variations of the exercise such as only have one leg on the swissball or favouring one arm in the pushup to make it the exercise harder.

Aim for 15 x reps for 3 x sets.

Place your shins on a Swiss ball and assume a pushup position, with your arms straight and your hands shoulder-width apart; this is the starting position.

Keeping your body straight, lower your chest until it nearly touches the floor, pause, and push back up as quickly as possible.

Next, roll the ball toward your chest by pulling it forward with both of your feet. Pause again, and then return to the starting position by lowering your hips and rolling the ball backward.

Tricep Dips

Aim to go as deep in the dip as possible to get the most out of the move.

Lift knees during the movement to add a core workout to the exercise.

By keeping your back straight and not leaning forward, you will work your triceps harder.

If you wish to work on your chest, leaning forward puts more emphasis on your pecs.

Aim for 15 x reps for 3 x sets.

Grip the dip bars with an overhand grip, keeping your elbows tucked in close to your body.

Allow your body weigh to hang so it is being supported by your arms and shoulders. Keep your hips straight.

Push down through your palms with your arms, lifting your body up until your arms are almost straight. (Do not lock your elbows)

Lower your body by slowly bending your elbows and continue down until you feel a slight stretch in your shoulders.

Pause, then push yourself back to the starting position.

Suspension Strap Press

Similar to the suspension strap pull this exercise can be made more difficult by placing feet on a swissball to bring the core into the exercise and balance.

Look to go deep into the press and change planes of movement to activate even more muscle during the exercise.

Aim for 20 x reps for 3 x sets.

Position yourself in a pushup position with the straps either side of your arms.

Walk your feet in under you while you grip the two straps before walking them back out until you are in the pushup position holding the straps.

Lower yourself bracing your core and press yourself back up to the starting position.

Consider placing a swissball under your feet for added difficulty.

Chapter 14: Advanced Kettlebell Workouts

In this chapter, I'm going to really ramp up your kettlebell training with advanced kettlebell workouts for your upper body, core, and lower body.

Before performing any of the workouts in the advanced workout chapter, practice the exercises without your kettlebell. Pay attention to how your body moves through the exercises and take note of any weaknesses or instabilities you may experience. Develop good form without the added weight of your kettlebell before you bring it into the workout. Good form is extremely important for getting the most out of your workout and preventing injuries.

Tip: It is a worthwhile idea to think about booking a session or two with an experienced kettlebell instructor to help you master your form in the advanced exercises. An experienced observer can watch your movement from an objective perspective and various angles, providing feedback and helping you perform each movement in an exercise with good form.

Important note: Many exercises throughout the workouts refer to placing your kettlebell in a racked position. Please refer to the explanation and image in Chapter 5 for beginners.

Lunges and Squats: Trouble knees are a common ailment and if you are affected, don't worry. If you are unable to perform full squats and lunges, only dip down as low as is comfortable for you. You can try taking the exercises further as you build your muscle strength. If not, just maintain the exercises at your own comfort level.

When to increase weight or reps: Please refer to Chapter 8 for guidelines on when to increase your kettlebell weight or repetitions and sets.

ADVANCED UPPER BODY KETTLEBELL WORKOUT

Bottoms up clean and press	8 - 10 per side	3 - 5
High pull	8 - 10 per side	3 - 5
Snatch	8 - 10 per side	3 - 5
Two-kettlebell military press	8 - 10	3 - 5
Push up with row	8 - 10 per side	3 - 5

Rest period between sets: 30 seconds to two minutes, decrease the rest time as you progress, and get fitter.

BOTTOMS UP CLEAN AND PRESS

Muscles targeted: Shoulders, back, core, quads, glutes, hamstrings

Stand with your feet shoulder-width apart, holding your kettlebell in the racked position but this time you are flipping your hell upside down so that the base faces upward. This is known as holding it bottoms up.

Extend your elbow and swing your kettlebell in a downward arc. As it is swinging downward, bend your knees and hinge your torso forward from your hips, allowing your kettlebell to swing between your legs.

As your kettlebell swings forward again, straighten your legs and torso back into a standing position. While straightening up, thrust your hips forward, the power from your hip thrust will add momentum to your kettlebell's upward swing.

As your kettlebell swings upwards, bend your elbow and bring it back into the racked position holding it bottoms up.

Extend your arm straight overhead to perform a press. Ensure that your arm is straight with your wrist, elbow, and shoulder in line with each other.

Return to the bottoms up racked position.

This exercise is exactly the same as the intermediate clean and press. The difficulty level is increased by holding your kettlebell bottoms up. This requires more grip strength and control of the bell to keep it balanced and prevent it flopping over.

Variation: Bottoms Up Clean and Push Press

Do more with your bottoms up clean and press by including a half squat. Perform your clean which will bring your kettlebell into the bottoms up racked position.

Before you perform the press, do a half squat. As you push up from the half squat to a standing position, use the momentum to extend your arm into the press.

Alternatively, you could perform the bottoms up clean and press with two kettlebells of the same weight for increased difficulty and weight.

HIGH PULL

Muscles targeted: shoulders, back, core, glutes, quads, hamstrings

This exercise is performed similarly to the single-handed kettlebell swing.

Stand with your feet shoulder-width apart, knees slightly bent, and torso hinged forward from the hips. Keep your back straight while your torso is hinged forward.

Grip the top of your kettlebell handle with one hand.

Lift your kettlebell off the ground and allow it to swing back between your legs.

Straighten up to a standing position, thrusting your hips forward. The hip thrust will offer momentum to your kettlebell swing.

Swing your kettlebell out in front of you in an arch until it reaches chest height while keeping your arm straight.

Once at chest height, pull your kettlebell backward toward you by bending your elbow while pulling your arm backward.

Push your kettlebell forward and allow it to descend into a downward swing.

As your kettlebell swings downward again, bend your knees and hinge your torso forward from the hips and allow the kettlebell to swing between your legs.

SNATCH

Muscles targeted: shoulders, back, forearms, glutes, hamstrings, quads

Stand with your feet shoulder-width apart, holding your kettlebell in the racked position.

Extend your elbow and swing your kettlebell in a downward arc. As it is swinging downward, bend your knees and hinge your torso forward from your hips, allowing your kettlebell to swing between your legs.

As your kettlebell swings forward again, straighten your legs and torso back into a standing position. While straightening up, thrust your hips forward, the power from your hip thrust will add momentum to your kettlebell's upward swing.

Maintaining a straight arm, bring your kettlebell all the way up, flipping it over as it travels upwards, until your arm is straight and your kettlebell is overhead.

Keeping your arm relatively straight, bring the kettlebell down in a swinging arc, bending your knees and hinging your torso forward from the hips, swinging it between your legs.

TWO-KETTLEBELL MILITARY PRESS

Muscles targeted: shoulders, back, triceps, core

Stand with your feet shoulder-width apart, one kettlebell in each hand, held in the racked position.

Extend both arms overhead to perform a double press. Ensure that your arms are straight with your wrists, elbows, and shoulders in line with each other.

Lower both kettlebells back to the racked position.

PUSH UP WITH ROW

Muscles targeted: shoulders, back, triceps, biceps, core

This exercise employs two kettlebells of the same weight.

Start in a push up position with each hand on the handle of a kettlebell and your arms straight.

Perform a push up and return to the starting position.

Raise one kettlebell off the floor by bending your elbow and pulling back towards the ceiling.

Lower your kettlebell by extending your arm downward, placing your kettlebell on the floor.

Raise one kettlebell off the floor by bending your elbow and pulling back towards the ceiling.

Lower your kettlebell by extending your arm downward, placing your kettlebell on the floor.

ADVANCED CORE KETTLEBELL WORKOUT

Turkish Get up	4 - 5 per side	3 - 5
Deck squat press	8 - 10	3 - 5
Walking renegade row	8 - 10 per side	3 - 5
Single-legged clean	8 - 10 per side	3 - 5
Side plank fly	8 - 10 per side	3 - 5

Rest period between sets: 30 seconds to two minutes, decrease the rest time as you progress, and get fitter.

TURKISH GET UP

Muscles targeted: core, shoulders, back, glutes, quads, hamstrings, hips, forearms

This exercise starts on the floor.

Lie on your right side with your kettlebell on your right next to your shoulder.

Use your right hand to grip the handle and your left hand to cradle the body of your kettlebell and roll over onto your back with your kettlebell.

As you roll over onto your back, press your right shoulder into the floor and extend your arm to raise the kettlebell and lock your elbow to maintain a straight arm.

Once you are lying on your back, place your left arm out to the side at a 45-degree angle to your body and bend your right knee, bringing your right foot as close to your bottom as you can.

Roll slightly to your left, bending your left elbow to help push your torso up off the floor. Don't roll over too much, just enough to push up with your left elbow. Maintain a straight right arm holding your kettlebell overhead.

Push up further with your left arm to straighten your elbow and support your weight with your hand flat on the floor.

Using your bent right leg, keep your foot flat on the ground and push your weight through your heel to raise your hips. For stability, extend your left leg as additional support.

Once your hips are raised, bring your left leg through under your right leg and body until you are in a half-kneeling position.

Use both legs to push up off the floor as if standing up from a lunge. Maintain a straight right arm with your kettlebell held overhead.

Each repetition of this exercise consists of the movement from the starting position on the floor through to the final standing position.

DECK SQUAT PRESS

Muscles targeted: Core, shoulders, back, hamstrings, glutes, quads

Stand with your feet shoulder-width apart, gripping your kettlebell by either side of the handle and holding it to your chest.

Bend your knees and hinge your torso forward from the hips to perform a squat.

From the squat position, gently lower your bottom further to the floor until you are in a sitting position, knees bent.

Lie back on the floor and push up through your heels to raise your hips to a glute bridge position.

As you raise your hips, lift your kettlebell upwards, away from your chest, and over your head until it is about an inch off the floor above your head.

Bring your kettlebell back over your head to your chest while you lower your hips back to the floor.

Bring yourself back into a sitting position before standing up again in one fluid motion.

Once you are in an upright standing position, raise your kettlebell overhead to perform a two-handed press.

Lower your kettlebell back to chest height.

WALKING RENEGADE ROW

Muscles targeted: core, shoulders, back, biceps, triceps

For this exercise, you will be using two kettlebells of the same weight.

Start in a push up or plank position with each hand on the handle of a kettlebell and your arms straight. Your kettlebells should be placed directly in line with your shoulders.

Using your right hand, pull your right side kettlebell up by bending your elbow and pulling back toward the ceiling.

When you lower your kettlebell back to the floor, place it slightly forward of where it was originally.

Step forward slightly with your left foot.

When you lower your kettlebell back to the floor, place it slightly forward of where it was originally.

When you lower your kettlebell back to the floor, place it slightly forward of your right side kettlebell.

Step forward slightly with your right foot.

SINGLE-LEGGED CLEAN

Muscles targeted: core, back, shoulders, hamstrings, quads

The single-legged clean is exactly the same as the basic clean except this time you are standing on only one leg instead of both legs.

Stand with your feet shoulder-width apart, holding your kettlebell in the racked position in your right hand. This is the same position that you will finish your repetition in.

Raise your right foot off the ground.

Extend your right elbow and drop your kettlebell downward. As you drop it downward, bend your left knee and hinge your torso forward from your hips, allowing your kettlebell to drop down to touch the ground.

Straighten up again and thrust your hips forward, the power from your hip thrust will add momentum to your kettlebell's upward swing.

As your kettlebell swings upwards, bend your elbow and bring it back into the racked position.

Always perform the clean on the side with the raised leg so that the weight of the bell acts as a counterweight for balance.

SIDE PLANK FLY

Muscles targeted: core, back, shoulders, quads, hamstrings

Start by lying on the floor on your side with your left elbow directly under your left shoulder in a straight line.

Place one foot on top of the other in a stacked position, legs straight and in line with your body.

Grip your kettlebell handle with your right hand. Lift it off the ground and flip it to bottoms up position where the base is pointing up to the ceiling or flip it all the way over so that it is resting against your outer forearm.

Extend your arm fully; raising your kettlebell toward the ceiling, locking your elbow, and making sure your shoulder is comfortable in the socket.

Using your core muscles, your left elbow under your shoulder, and your legs, raise your hips off the floor towards the ceiling. You should be in a side plank position.

If the side plank position is too challenging with your feet stacked one on top of the other, place one foot in front of the other for increased stability.

Hold the side plank position, kettlebell raised toward the ceiling, for 30 seconds.

Lower your hips to the floor and bring your kettlebell back to the floor.

ADVANCED LOWER BODY KETTLEBELL WORKOUT

Alternating kettlebell swing	8 - 10 per hand	3 - 5
Clean, squat, press	8 - 10 per side	3 - 5
Pistol squat	8 - 10 per side	3 - 5
Tactical lunge	8 - 10 per	3 - 5

		side	
Lunge row		8 - 10 per side	3 - 5

Rest period between sets: 30 seconds to two minutes, decrease the rest time as you progress, and get fitter.

ALTERNATING KETTLEBELL SWING

Stand with your feet shoulder-width apart, knees slightly bent, and torso hinged forward from the hips. Keep your back straight while your torso is hinged forward.

Grip the top of your kettlebell handle with one hand.

Lift your kettlebell off the ground and allow it to swing back between your legs.

Straighten up to a standing position, thrusting your hips forward. The hip thrust will offer momentum to your kettlebell swing.

Swing your kettlebell out in front of you in an arc until it reaches chest height while keeping your arm straight.

At chest height or just as your kettlebell begins its descent, pass it to the other hand.

As your kettlebell swings downward again, bend your knees and hinge your torso forward from the hips and allow the kettlebell to swing between your legs.

CLEAN, SQUAT, PRESS

Muscles targeted: glutes, hamstrings, quads, core, shoulders, back

Stand with your feet shoulder-width apart, holding your kettlebell in the racked position. This is the same position that you will finish your repetition in.

Extend your elbow and swing your kettlebell in a downward arc. As it is swinging downward, bend your knees and hinge your torso forward from your hips, allowing your kettlebell to swing between your legs.

As your kettlebell swings forward again, straighten your legs and torso back into a standing position. While straightening up, thrust your hips forward, the power from your hip thrust will add momentum to your kettlebell's upward swing.

As your kettlebell swings upwards, bend your elbow and bring it back into the racked position.

Bend your knees and hinge your torso forward from the hips to perform a squat.

Return to a standing position.

From the racked position, extend your arm straight overhead to perform a press. Ensure that your arm is straight with your wrist, elbow, and shoulder in line with each other.

Bring your kettlebell back to the racked position.

PISTOL SQUAT

Muscles targeted: quads, glutes, hamstrings, shoulders, core

Stand with your feet shoulder-width apart, gripping your kettlebell on either side of the handle and holding it to your chest.

Raise your left foot off the floor.

Push down through your right heel, keeping your foot flat on the floor. Do not shift your weight onto the ball of your foot or lift your heel off the floor.

Bend your right knee, hinging at the hips, to squat down on your right leg.

As you squat down with your right leg, extend your left leg out in front of you, keeping your left foot off the floor. At the same time, extend your arms out in front of you so that your kettlebell is acting as a counterweight to help maintain balance.

The pistol squat is a very deep squat, lower yourself as close to the floor as possible.

Come out of the squat position by pushing up through your heel, extending and straightening your right knee, and bringing your kettlebell closer to your chest.

Tip: If the pistol squat is too challenging, try performing it with your back against a wall for extra support while you build your strength, balance, and muscle control.

TACTICAL LUNGE

Muscles targeted: quads, glutes, hamstrings, core, shoulders

Stand with your feet shoulder-width apart. Grip your kettlebell with your right hand, letting it hang at your side.

Step into a lunge position by either stepping back into a reverse lunge or forward into a regular lunge.

Ensure that your right leg is the leg that is behind you.

Hold the lunge position and pass your kettlebell under your left leg from your right hand to your left hand.

Return to a standing position and repeat the exercise from left to right.

LUNGE ROW

Muscles targeted: glutes, hamstrings, quads, back, core, shoulders

Stand with your feet shoulder-width apart. Grip your kettlebell with your right hand, letting it hang at your side.

Step into a lunge position by either stepping back into a reverse lunge or forward into a regular lunge.

Instead of a full lunge, you are going to bend the front knee and keep the back leg straight behind you. Ensure that the leg that is extended behind you is your right leg, the same side that you are holding the kettlebell.

Use your left elbow to support your upper body by leaning on your left thigh.

Pull your kettlebell towards your ribs by bending your elbow as you pull your elbow backward and up toward the ceiling.

Lower your kettlebell by extending your arm toward the floor.

Conclusion

The Kettlebell as a weight may have been around for centuries, but it's only since the early 1960s that the west has even realized that such a versatile piece of equipment exists. Even then, it took us almost 30 years to finally start putting the Kettlebell to good use. Ever since, this metal marvel has helped countless of American fitness enthusiasts gain serious growth in strength and muscle, some of those have achieved that strength yet kept their toned body. Others have gained muscle definition like those displayed by ancient Greek and Roman statues.

Whatever you may be, be you amateur or professional, or just a gym enthusiast, the kettlebell is an essential part of kit that you just cannot do without. With a kettlebell and this book, you shall have you all the tools needed to enable you to work out to your full potential. These easy to learn techniques are just the beginning of the things you can do with a kettlebell. As the weight has its origins in the fields, there are countless other exercises that you can learn, and countless others you can work with.

Just remember that as much as you're training, you also have to train smart. Give your body's different muscle groups time to recuperate from workout sessions, do not over work yourself, and above all, make sure that your posture and form through all these exercises is correct to avoid injury. If you feel unsure about certain stances and postures, remember, there is no shame in asking for professional help. Safety, whether at home, at the park or at the gym should be the highest priority.